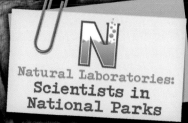

Natural Laboratories:
Scientists in
National Parks

CARLSBAD
CAVERNS

Robin Koontz

Educational Media

rourkeeducationalmedia.com

Before, During, and After Reading Activities

Before Reading: Building Background Knowledge and Academic Vocabulary

"Before Reading" strategies activate prior knowledge and set a purpose for reading. Before reading a book, it is important to tap into what your child or students already know about the topic. This will help them develop their vocabulary and increase their reading comprehension.

Questions and activities to build background knowledge:
1. Look at the cover of the book. What will this book be about?
2. What do you already know about the topic?
3. Let's study the Table of Contents. What will you learn about in the book's chapters?
4. What would you like to learn about this topic? Do you think you might learn about it from this book? Why or why not?

Building Academic Vocabulary

Building academic vocabulary is critical to understanding subject content.
Assist your child or students to gain meaning of the following vocabulary words.
Content Area Vocabulary
Read the list. What do these words mean?

- antibiotics
- extremophiles
- fossilized
- guano
- gypsum
- hydromagnesite
- infrared
- insecticide
- limestone
- microorganisms
- paleontologists
- stalactites

During Reading: Writing Component

"During Reading" strategies help to make connections, monitor understanding, generate questions, and stay focused.
1. While reading, write in your reading journal any questions you have or anything you do not understand.
2. After completing each chapter, write a summary of the chapter in your reading journal.
3. While reading, make connections with the text and write them in your reading journal.
   a) Text to Self – What does this remind me of in my life? What were my feelings when I read this?
   b) Text to Text – What does this remind me of in another book I've read? How is this different from other books I've read?
   c) Text to World – What does this remind me of in the real world? Have I heard about this before? (News, current events, school, etc....)

After Reading: Comprehension and Extension Activity

"After Reading" strategies provide an opportunity to summarize, question, reflect, discuss, and respond to text. After reading the book, work on the following questions with your child or students to check their level of reading comprehension and content mastery.
1. What kinds of things are researchers studying at Carlsbad Caverns National Park? (Summarize)
2. What would be difficult about exploring a cave? (Infer)
3. What do scientists learn about climate change by exploring the caverns? (Asking Questions)
4. What would you research if you had permission to explore Lechuguilla Cave? (Text to Self Connection)

Extension Activity
A cave map includes dimensions and details about formations and other features. Imagine a cave you are exploring. Draw an outline of it and identify all the features and measurements.

TABLE OF CONTENTS

CHAPTER ONE

DESERT DISCOVERY

The Chihuahuan Desert covers nearly 200,000 square miles (518,000 square kilometers) of area in New Mexico, Texas, Arizona, and Mexico. The largest desert in North America, it contains or is next to several mountain ranges, including the Guadalupe Mountains.

Chihuahuan Desert

Guadalupe Mountains

Desert Valley in Big Bend area

American Indians were the original explorers and settlers in the area that later became Carlsbad Caverns National Park. The Mescalero Apache, Zuni Pueblo, and other tribes that lived along the desert's northern edge knew about the incredible **limestone** world that existed hundreds of feet below.

The Mescalero Apache people were nomadic hunters and gatherers living in the southwestern United States.

"Caves are like time capsules offering clues from the formation of the planet to the beginning of human civilization."

— *Rod Horrocks, Cave Specialist at Carlsbad Caverns National Park*

But some of the largest, longest, deepest, and most beautiful caverns on Earth went unnoticed by European settlers until a young cowboy witnessed a spectacle unlike any he'd ever seen.

Carlsbad Canyon

As the story goes, in 1898, 16-year-old James Larkin White was looking for stray cattle. Off in the distance, he saw a huge funnel of bats swirling out of the desert hills. There were so many bats it looked like a volcano billowing smoke into the sky.

James
Larkin White
July 11, 1882 –
April 26, 1946

When they emerge from Carlsbad Cave, the Brazilian free-tailed bats usually head

Early explorers had no idea what lay below as they climbed down handmade wood and wire ladders.

Jim soon discovered "the biggest and blackest hole I had ever seen, out of which the bats seemed literally to boil." The young cowboy had discovered the entrance to Carlsbad Cavern, which became the main attraction at Carlsbad Caverns National Park. Jim was the premier explorer of the caverns, entering the massive cave with a ladder he created from wire and wood. He devoted much of his life to exploring the caverns and harvesting massive amounts of bat **guano** for fertilizer.

The park was established in 1930 and is one of the few protected areas within the Chihuahuan Desert ecosystem. Much of the scientific research underway there takes place in the caverns of the park.

cave entrance

CHAPTER TWO

A SUBTERRANEAN WORLD

It wasn't until the 1970s that geologists discovered how the limestone caves had formed in the Guadalupe Mountains. About 250 million years ago, the entire area was underneath an ancient sea with hundreds of miles of limestone reefs along its shore. These barrier reefs are called the Capitan Reef Complex.

Early surveyors used the National Geographic Pit to access the Lower Cave.

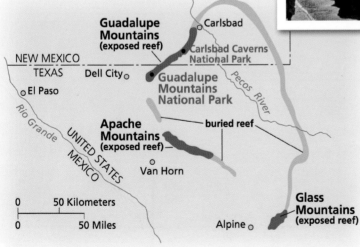

Map of Capitan Reef Complex

As the sea evaporated, the reef complex uplifted and eroded. Hydrogen sulfide from oil deposits mixed with

Sulfuric acid

microbes and oxygen in ancient water to form sulfuric acid. Though most limestone caves are formed from the carbonic acid in the water flowing through them, geologists discovered that it was sulfuric acid that created the Carlsbad Caverns.

exposed reef

Over millions of years, the acid melted away massive chambers and tunnels in the limestone. The exposed part of the reef became part of the Guadalupe Mountains.

inside Carlsbad Cavern

karst system

Karst Systems

Other kinds of caves were formed by rainwater that sank through cracks in the ground. This created underground streams and rivers as it dissolved the surrounding limestone. Caves like this are called karst systems. The caves that formed in the Guadalupe Mountains have very few karst features because of the way they

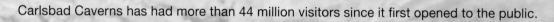
Carlsbad Caverns has had more than 44 million visitors since it first opened to the public.

Jim White was the first to explore the cave. But, in time, more explorers joined him. Their main goals in the early years were to map the massive cave system and make it more accessible to tourists and scientists.

Chandelier Ballroom of Lechuguilla Cave

Any kind of cave research requires cave cartography, which is creating a map of the cave. Cave mapping shows the routes between rooms and passageways. Mapping also includes information about the cave's features, including historical evidence and biological observation.

Dripping water creates a variety of decorations on the cave floor, including stalagmites.

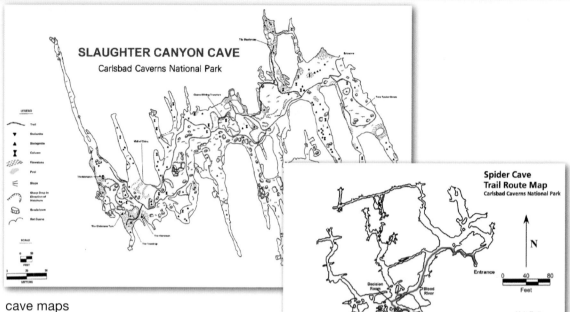
cave maps

Survey groups have mapped the Carlsbad Cavern and other caves in the park since the 1960s. Surveyors used instruments such as measuring tapes; inclinometers to measure tilt, elevation, or depression of objects; and compasses along with tools for sketching.

Soda straws are hollow mineral tubes. They are also called tubular stalactites.

A team usually had four people assigned for a mapping expedition. One handled instrument control, one sketched, one measured, and the fourth took inventory of the cave features. The researchers combined all their data into notebooks.

Waterproof clothing, boots, gloves, helmet, and kneepads help make cave exploration more comfortable and safe.

Cave mappers still use handwritten notes and drawings to record their findings.

Cave mapping done in the late 1980s included logging data into a computer mapping program and database. By then, laser distance meters mostly replaced measuring tapes.

The scanner slowly orbits on a tripod, producing super-detailed 3D views of the cavern's profile.

Laser imaging and 3D scanning are the newest technologies used in cave mapping. In 2018, researchers from the University of Arkansas created a three-dimensional digital map of the Carlsbad Cavern. The team used a light-detection and ranging tool called LiDAR. Pulsed laser collected billions of measurements that digitally recreated the space.

CHAPTER THREE

CAVE GEOLOGY

Only the Carlsbad Cavern is open to the public. Other caves in the park can be entered by permit with specific guidelines about clothing, gear, and procedures. The goal is to conserve and protect the cave environments and minimize human impacts.

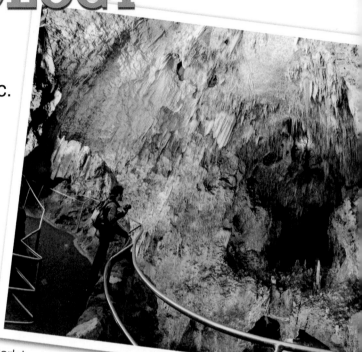

Carlsbad Cavern has pathways and handrails for visitors as a way to keep them and the cave features safe.

Visitors walk the path to Carlsbad Cavern entrance.

Doing so provides a living laboratory for geologists, biologists, and other researchers to study a range of topics while preserving the ancient wilderness.

Lint Collectors

In recent years, volunteers pick and collect lint, clothing fibers, and hair from the thousands of tourists that visit the caverns. Lint can upset a cave's ecosystem by hosting non-native **microorganisms.** *It can also trap carbon dioxide, which can dissolve cave formations.*

Lechuguilla Cave has features not found in any other cave in the world. A natural collapse just inside its entrance hid it from explorers for thousands of years.

gypsum flower in Lechuguilla Cave

inside Lechuguilla Cave

Since its discovery in 1986, Lechuguilla Cave has been closed to the public. A few scientific and exploration teams are allowed access for research.

Cave Specialist

A speleologist studies the structures, history, physical properties, and life forms in caves and other limestone landscape features, including how they slowly change over time. Carlsbad is popular with speleologists because it is still in a state of formation after 250 million years.

Lechuguilla Cave is sometimes called the "Jewel of the Underground." The cave's great depth gives geologists rare views of the geologic formations of the ancient Capitan Reef Complex.

cave pearls inside Lechuguilla

It takes a lot of hiking, slithering, and rope descents to reach Lake Lebarge deep inside Lechuguilla Cave.

Geologists have discovered a wide variety of geologic features, some not visible in any other cave in the world. Unlike most caves, Lechuguilla Cave built itself from the bottom up, rather than the top down.

Lily pads are formed when calcite drips into a pool. They can grow downward, forming a pedestal that holds them in place even when the water recedes.

The speleothems include chandeliers formed from pure **gypsum** that are 20 feet (6 meters) long; draperies; columns; popcorn; "hairs and beards"; soda straws; **hydromagnesite** balloons; and thousands of calcite cave pearls shaped from running water.

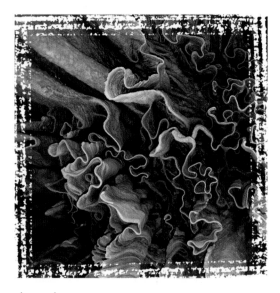

draperies

chandeliers

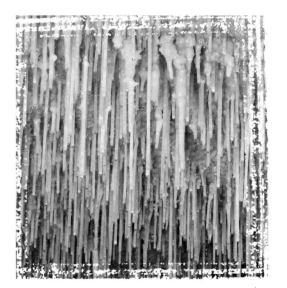

soda straws

cave popcorn

Cave Decorations

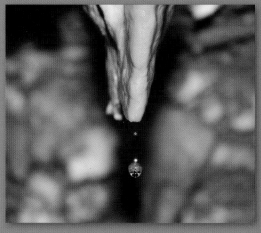

cave calcium drip

Rain and melting snow that soak into the limestone mix with gases and minerals in the air and soil. As the water evaporates, tiny amounts of a mineral called calcite are left behind. Drip by drip, cave formations called speleothems grow.

Deep in the cave around Lake Castrovalva, one of many lakes in the cavern, there are massive **stalactites** in pastel colors. Biologists and geologists recently discovered that this lifeless-looking cave is teeming with an incredible microscopic animal community. They also discovered these animals have much to do with the geologic formations the scientists admired.

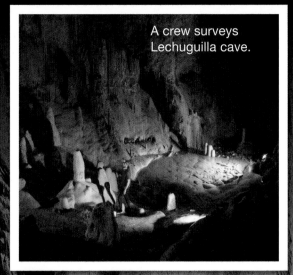

A crew surveys Lechuguilla cave.

Pearlsian Gulf in Lechuguilla Cave

The Endless Cave

As of 2017, researchers had surveyed and photographed 142 miles (228 kilometers) of Lechuguilla Cave at depths down to 1,604 feet (489 meters). And there is still more to explore!

CHAPTER FOUR

CAVE DWELLERS

Lechuguilla Cave is the deepest cave in the United States. It takes thousands of years for surface water to seep into the depths of its caverns. Because of its extreme isolation, Lechuguilla Cave has its own unique ecosystem.

Formations called soda straws hang in Lechuguilla Cave.

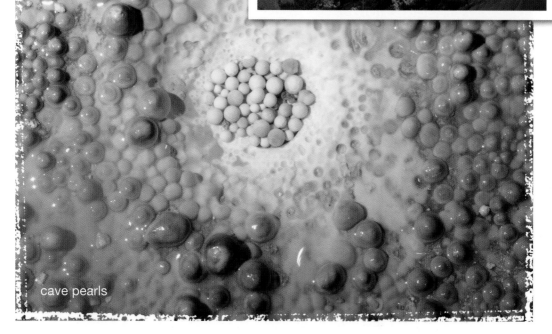

cave pearls

Earlier explorers at first assumed that nothing lived in Lechuguilla Cave because there are no food sources. But they were wrong! Millions of microbes live in the cave, feeding on the minerals. Scientists found that microscopic bacteria play a big role in the formation of the caves and its diverse speleothems. And there's even more to the story of these amazing **extremophiles**.

Scientists recently found an ancient microbe in the cave that has been isolated from people for millions of years.

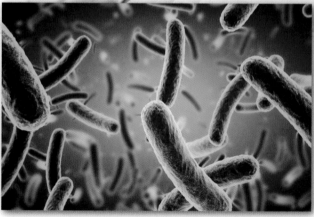

Microbiologists recently discovered that even though these bacteria have been isolated for millions of years, they are resistant to all **antibiotics** we've developed so far. That resistance allows the bacteria to survive attacks by other microorganisms. Studying these organisms may help medical researchers find new antibiotics for future disease-causing bacteria.

Other bacteria found only in Lechuguilla Cave have given scientists promising leads in the development of drugs that fight cancer.

Microbiologists come to the Carlsbad Caverns to study the microbial life that thrives deep inside.

Life on Other Planets

NASA scientists visited Lechuguilla Cave to study the extremophiles. The way these mineral-eating bacteria survive may give them clues about how life could survive on other planets.

Bats fly out of Carlsbad Cavern.

There are 17 species of bats in Carlsbad Caverns National Park. The most famous are the bats Jim White saw, called Brazilian free-tailed bats. According to evidence found by explorers, the mostly female bats have occupied the caverns for at least 5,000 years.

There are also bats roosting in backcountry caves and in the trees. Small numbers of cave myotis and fringed myotis bats roost in other areas of the cave away from the free-tailed bats.

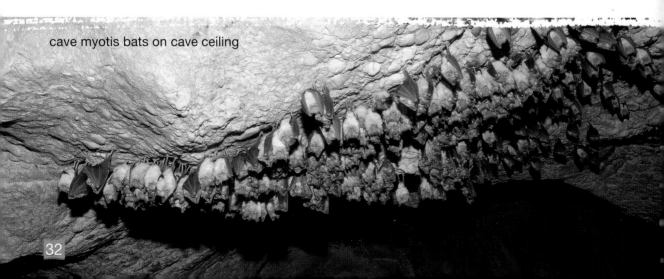

cave myotis bats on cave ceiling

cave myotis bat

The cave-dwelling bats are insectivores, eating insects such as moths, mosquitoes, and beetles. During spring and summer, the cave serves as their daytime roost site for sleeping, a night roost, and a maternity site.

Amazing Exits and Entries

Bats fly counterclockwise out of the mouth of the cave when they exit. They return one at a time, just before dawn, folding their wings and diving into the cave with a whoosh!

A worker sprays DDT on plants.

The number of free-tail bats in the Carlsbad colony has decreased from several million to about 500,000 bats. To find out why, researchers studied preserved specimens from the previous 50 years. They concluded that an **insecticide** called DDT played a major role in the decline. Though DDT was banned in the U.S. in 1972, Mexico continued to spray areas where the bats spent their winters until 2000.

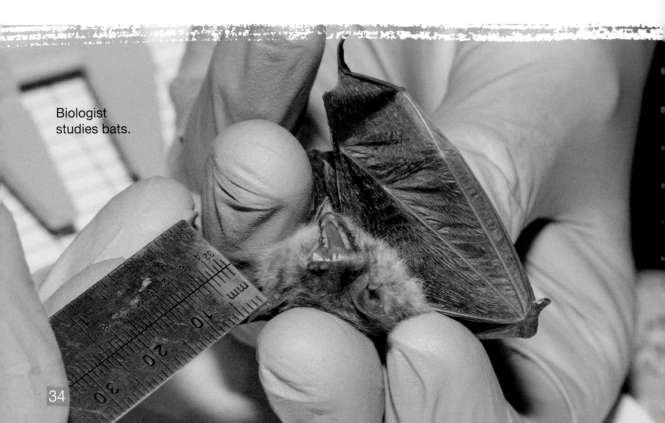

Biologist studies bats.

thermal infrared image of bats

To record population changes, researchers use thermal **infrared** imaging cameras that reveal the bats' heat signatures. A computer program counts and records the number of signatures in the photographs.

Deadly Disease

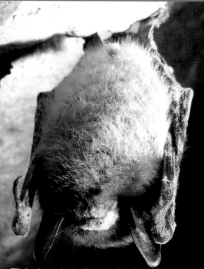

This bat is infected with White-nose Syndrome.

Scientists are studying a disease affecting bat colonies called White-nose Syndrome (WNS). WNS is considered the worst wildlife disease to hit North America. It has killed millions of bats. So far, the bats in Carlsbad Caverns National Park have not been infected. Scientists think bats are infected during hibernation, and the Carlsbad Cavern bats do not hibernate. Still, biologists continue monitoring the health of Carlsbad bats.

When cave swallows enter the Carlsbad Cavern, they float down into the entrance in a spiral.

One of the largest colonies of cave swallows in the U.S. also raises young in Carlsbad Cavern. They build mud nests in the entrance to the cave. Like the bats, swallows hunt insects in flight.

Since 1980, the swallows have been banded as part of a research project to study their lives and migration patterns. Their winter range was unknown until the banding project revealed Carlsbad Cavern swallows living on the Pacific coast of Mexico.

migrating swallow

Bird Banding

Banding is one of the earliest scientific methods used to track migratory animals such as birds. It was first used by biologist Hans Christian C. Mortensen in 1890. The recovery of banded birds helps identify migration patterns.

CHAPTER FIVE

FOSSIL HISTORY

Fossils are important to scientists as a way to piece together the history of life on Earth. As Earth's climate changes, studying how previous life survived—or perished—helps scientists devise ways to predict the future of our planet.

marine fossil in southwest desert

Salt Basin Dunes in Guadalupe Mountains National Park

The end of the Permian period was the end of the Paleozoic era, more than 250 million years ago. It is the largest known mass extinction in Earth's history. Marine life suffered the most during this time, and most of the reef builders became extinct. Fossils from that period help geologists understand the ancient environment.

A chisel-edge rock hammer works well in the exposed ancient reef. The square head breaks apart rock, and the chisel edge is used to split apart layers of sedimentary rock.

Exploring and studying the rocks at Carlsbad Caverns National Park allows scientists to reconstruct the climate record for the Holocene and late Pleistocene periods in the southwestern U.S.

The Permian-age reef of the Carlsbad Caverns National Park was constructed almost entirely from dead marine animals such as sponges and algae. The **fossilized** ocean creatures captured in the massive reef system are some of the best preserved in the world.

Marine animals, including ammonites, snails, trilobites, and brachiopods, make the fossil reef a gold mine to **paleontologists**. Explorers have also discovered and unearthed about 36 species of vertebrate fossils.

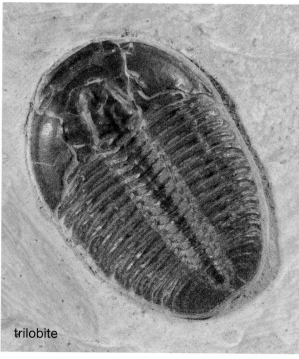

trilobite

Equus
(ancient horse)

In recent years, paleontologists from Texas Tech University and the Smithsonian Institution found animal fossils, including *Equus* (ancient horse), *Bassariscus* (ringtail), a wolf, and a cat similar to modern day bobcats.

Fossil Fuel

Geologists also study the rocks and fossils in the Guadalupe Mountains to learn more about where and how petroleum deposits are formed and how to access them to produce fossil fuels.

43

Scientific exploration continues in the vast depths and lengths of the Carlsbad Caverns. With more than 119 caves discovered so far, investigation teams map more and more of Carlsbad Caverns' ancient underground wilderness. Their reports continue to reveal amazing mysteries and always, new questions for scientists to ponder.

MAKE A SPELEOTHEM

Demonstrate how speleothems are formed in caves by making your own cave formation. Using concentrated Epsom salt will speed up a process that usually takes hundreds of years.

Supplies

- 2 cups (480 milliliters) Epsom salt (magnesium sulfate)
- 2 clear small jars
- 1 cup (240 milliliters) warm water
- small plate or a tray made from aluminum foil
- spoon
- 30 inches (76.2 centimeters) cotton string or yarn
- 2 paper clips

Directions:

1. Slowly stir 1 cup (240 milliliters) of Epsom salt, a spoonful at a time, into 1/2 cup (120 milliliters) of warm water in each jar. Make sure it is completely dissolved.

2. Tie the paperclips on either end of the string, then dip in the salt solution, making sure it is completely saturated.

3. Place the tray between the cups, then bridge the string between the two cups, making sure both ends are submerged in each cup and the middle of the string is lower than the solution levels in each cup.

4. Place a little bit of Epsom salt on the tray. Leave the cups in a sunny place if possible for a couple of days without moving them.

Glossary

antibiotics (an-ti-bye-OT-iks): drugs, such as penicillin, that kill bacteria and are used to cure infections and diseases

extremophiles (ek-STREEM-oh-files): organisms adapted to living in extreme conditions

fossilized (FOSS-uhl-ized): when an ancient plant or animal is preserved as rock

guano (GWAH-no): the excrement of seabirds and bats, used as fertilizer

gypsum (JIP-suhm): a mineral made of hydrated calcium sulfate

hydromagnesite (HYE-druh-mag-nuh-site): a mineral made of a basic magnesium carbonate in the form of small white crystals or chalky crusts

infrared (in-fruh-RED): located outside the visible spectrum at its red end

insecticide (in-SEK-tuh-side): a chemical used to kill insects

limestone (LIME-stohn): a hard rock formed from the remains of shells or coral

microorganisms (mye-kroh-OR-guh-niz-uhms): living things that are too small to be seen without a microscope

paleontologists (pale-ee-uhn-TOL-uh-jists): scientists who deal with fossils and other ancient life forms

stalactites (stuh-LAK-tites): thin pieces of rock shaped like icicles that hang from the roof of a cave

Index

Show What You Know

1. What is unusual about the way the caverns in Carlsbad Caverns National Park were formed?

2. What is a karst system?

3. Why is it important to try to keep foreign substances away from the caverns?

4. What are three types of speleothems in the caverns other than stalagmites and stalactites?

5. What is considered the worst wildlife disease to ever hit North America?

Further Reading

Aulenbach, Nancy Holler and Barton, Hazel A., *Exploring Caves: Journeys into the Earth*, National Geographic Children's Books, 2001.

Reames, Stephen, *Deep Secrets: The Discovery and Exploration of Lechuguilla Cave*, Cave Books, 1999.

Thompson, Doug, *Underground Ranger: Adventures in Carlsbad Caverns National Park and Other Remarkable Places*, University of New Mexico Press, 2016.

About the Author

Robin Koontz is a freelance author/illustrator of a wide variety of nonfiction and fiction books, educational blogs, and magazine articles for children and young adults. Her 2011 science title, *Leaps and Creeps: How Animals Move to Survive*, was an Animal Behavior Society Outstanding Children's Book Award Finalist. Raised in Maryland and Alabama, Robin now lives with her husband in the Coast Range of western Oregon where she especially enjoys observing the wildlife on her property. You can learn more on her blog: robinkoontz.wordpress.com.

Meet The Author!
www.meetREMauthors.com

www.rourkeeducationalmedia.com

PHOTO CREDITS: Cover foreground photo 2By Blazej Lyjak/Shutterstock.com, cover bkground photo and title page © Galyna Andrushko/Shutterstock.com, card with paper clip art © beths/Shutterstock.com; contents page ©William Silver/Shutterstock.com; PAGE 4-5: Pingebat, Maxine Weiss, Maxine Weiss, RobertWaltman, Randall, A. Frank. PAGE 6-7: courtesy of Carlsbad Caverns National Park, Courtesy National Park Service, Zack Frank. PAGE 8-9: kurtlichtenstein, National Park Service Photo/Peter Jones, Courtsey National Park Service. PAGE 10-11: RobertWaltman, petroudny43, elan7t50, Aleksejs Bergmanis, molekuul_be. PAGE 12-13 JHVEPhoto, Breck P. Kent, National Park Service. PAGE 14-15: pakorn sungkapukdee, Shawn Thomas/National Park Service, Gilitukha,. PAGE 16-17: Lithiumphoto, University of Arkansas/CAST; PAGE 18-19: Crackerclips | Dreamstime.com, pabst_ell, mihtiander, National Park Service. PAGE 20-21: Salajean | Dreamstime.com, National Park Service Photo/Jean Krejca, NPS Photo/Gavin Newman. PAGE 22-23: National Park Service Photo/Gavin Newman, NPS Photo/Jean Krejca, NPS Photo/Daniel Chailloux & Peter Bosted. PAGE 24-25: National Park Service Photo/Shawn Thomas, Credit: NPS Photo/Gavin Newman, rile14, arinahabich, Joseph Alger. PAGE 26-27: National Park Service Photo/Gavin Newman, NPS Photo/Jean Krejca, Dave Bunnell- Creative Commons Attribution-Share Alike 2.5 Generic license. PAGE 28-29: National Park Service Photo/Shawn Thomas, Attribution: WTucker at the English Wikipedia- CCA Share Alike 3.0 Unported license., Giovanni Cancemi. Page 29 inset of microbe © Prof. Eshel Ben-Jaco https://creativecommons.org/licenses/by-sa/3.0/deed.en PAGE 30-31: science photo, paulista, salajean/ Shutterstock.com, Gennady Kudashev | Dreamstime.com, benkrut. PAGE 32-33: Jason Mintzer, Cucu Remus, Phil Degginger/ Alamy Stock Photo, Beth Ruggiero-York, kyslynskahal, Navigatia. PAGE 34-35: salajean, GrooTrai, National Science Foundation -Thomas Kunz, Boston University, Marvin Moriarty/USFWS, ivansmuk. PAGE 36-37: Alan Schmierer- Creative Commons CC0 1.0 Universal Public Domain Dedication, Maksimilian. PAGE 38-39: Rocket Photos - HQ Stock, Solianova Margarita, ArtyAlison. PAGE 40-41: crazymedia, Breck P. Kent, Aneese, arinahabich. PAGE 42-43: Breck P. Kent, James St. John-Attribution 2.0 Generic (CC BY 2.0), Trifonov_Evgeniy, Digital_Lions. PAGE 44-45: megasquib. www.shutterstock.com, www.istock.com, www.dreamstime.com

Edited by: Keli Sipperley

Produced by Blue Door Education for Rourke Educational Media. Cover design by: Nicola Stratford; Interior design and layout by: Jennifer Dydyk

Carlsbad Caverns / Robin Koontz
(Natural Laboratories: Scientists in National Parks)
ISBN 978-1-64369-023-0 (hard cover)
ISBN 978-1-64369-117-6 (soft cover)
ISBN 978-1-64369-170-1 (e-Book)
Library of Congress Control Number: 2018956032

Printed in the United States of America, North Mankato, Minnesota